YELLOWSTONE
NATIONAL PARK

by Ruth Radlauer

Design and photographs
by Rolf Zillmer

AN ELK GROVE BOOK

 CHILDRENS PRESS ™

CHICAGO

Bequest of Beauty

A bequest is a gift for those who follow. Each National Park is a BEQUEST OF BEAUTY. It is a place of special interest or beauty that has been saved by the United States government especially for you, your children, and their great-great-grandchildren. This bequest is yours to have and to care for so that others who follow can do the same during their lives.

With gratitude for Tracy and Ruth Shaw

Photo credits: pages 27 (all but paintbrush) and page 45 (lower left) courtesy of Norman A. Bishop, Yellowstone National Park.

Library of Congress Cataloging in Publication Data

Radlauer, Ruth Shaw.
   Yellowstone National Park.

   (National parks, bequest of beauty series)
   "An Elk Grove book."
   SUMMARY: Brief text and photographs present the geographic features, plant and animal life, and other attractions of the first national park.
   1. Yellowstone National Park—Juvenile literature.
[1. Yellowstone National Park] I. Zillmer, Rolf, ill.
II. Title. III. Series.
F722.R32   917.87'52'043   75-2159
ISBN 0-516-07487-3

      7 8 9 10 11 12 13 14 15 R 91 90 89 88 87 86 85

917.87
RAD
1985

Contents

Yellowstone, a Place of Wonder

You are in a place that seems like a dream. You hear strange rumbles, and steam spouts from the ground. You look up at some pink and white steps to see wisps of steam. It's a place of wonder!

Here you can wander through "fossil forests." The trees in the forests are petrified, turned into stone.

Where are you? You're in Yellowstone National Park.

Waterfalls drop into deep canyons of yellow rock, and swans and ducks swim on the lakes.

Green, growing forests of lodgepole pine, spruce, and fir shelter squirrels, chipmunks, and bears. Thousands of elk and bison graze in grassy meadows.

Yellowstone is a place to ride horses, go fishing, and hike on boardwalk nature trails through geyser basins.

It's cold nights around the campfire and frosty mornings when you run to keep warm. This is Yellowstone, the first National Park in the world.

Riverside Geyser

Petrified Tree

Minerva Terrace

Lower Yellowstone Fall

Have a Safe Trip

To help your family plan a trip to this wonderland, you can write for information to the Reservations and Activities Departments at TW Services, Inc., Yellowstone National Park, Wyoming, 82190.

Here are some ways to plan a safe trip to Yellowstone:

1. Remind adults to drive carefully and watch for bicycles and motorcycles. A stopped car should never block the road and needs to be locked when left even for a minute.

2. The best way to view wildlife is from a distance, so binoculars are nice to have. Small animals can carry disease, so feeding or touching them is not allowed.

3. If you camp, plan to keep food locked in the car or suspended 10 feet above the ground to avoid attracting bears.

4. Bison and elk may look friendly, but they may charge and hurt you with horns or heavy hooves. Watch them from a distance.

5. Be careful around water. Look at waterfalls from protected areas where viewing is best. See page 18.

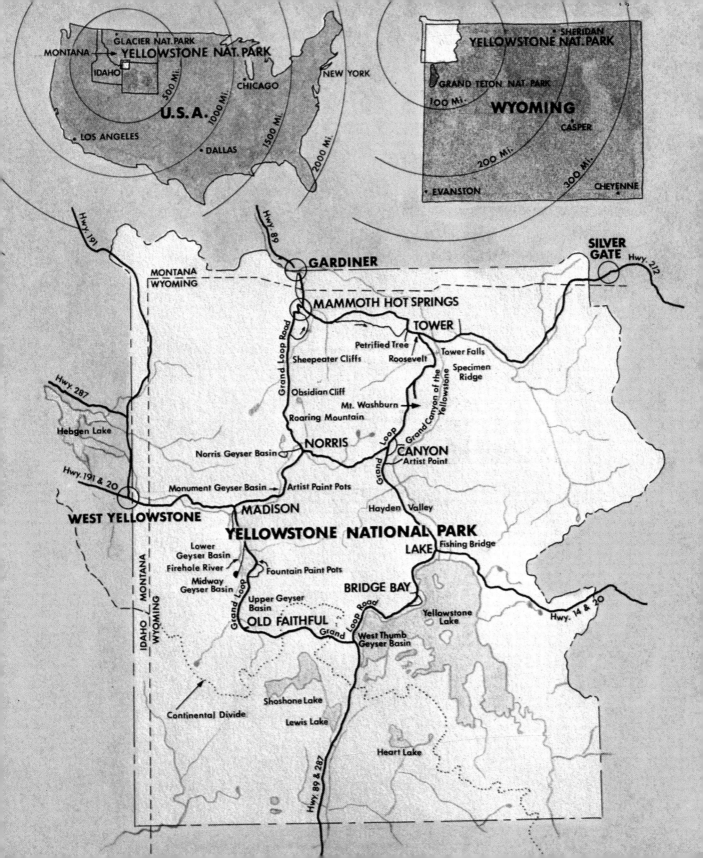

U.S.A.

MONTANA

GLACIER NAT. PARK

YELLOWSTONE NAT. PARK

IDAHO

500 Mi.

1000 Mi.

1500 Mi.

2000 Mi.

NEW YORK

CHICAGO

LOS ANGELES

DALLAS

YELLOWSTONE NAT. PARK

SHERIDAN

WYOMING

GRAND TETON NAT. PARK

100 Mi.

200 Mi.

300 Mi.

CASPER

EVANSTON

CHEYENNE

Hwy. 191

Hwy. 89

GARDINER

SILVER GATE

Hwy. 212

MONTANA
WYOMING

MAMMOTH HOT SPRINGS

TOWER

Petrified Tree

Tower Falls

Sheepeater Cliffs

Roosevelt

Specimen Ridge

Grand Loop Road

Obsidian Cliff

Mt. Washburn

Roaring Mountain

Grand Canyon of the Yellowstone

Hwy. 287

Hebgen Lake

NORRIS

CANYON

Artist Point

Norris Geyser Basin

Grand Loop

Hwy. 191 & 20

Monument Geyser Basin

Artist Paint Pots

WEST YELLOWSTONE

MADISON

Hayden Valley

YELLOWSTONE NATIONAL PARK

LAKE

Fishing Bridge

Lower Geyser Basin

Firehole River

Fountain Paint Pots

Midway Geyser Basin

BRIDGE BAY

IDAHO
MONTANA
WYOMING

Upper Geyser Basin

Grand Loop

OLD FAITHFUL

Grand Loop Road

West Thumb Geyser Basin

Yellowstone Lake

Hwy. 14 & 20

Continental Divide

Shoshone Lake

Lewis Lake

Hwy. 89 & 287

Heart Lake

A Look Inside the Earth

A visit to Yellowstone National Park helps you understand some of the things going on inside the earth.

Everywhere in the park, hot places called *thermal areas* show us that there were great volcanic eruptions here during three different periods in the past two million years. Another reminder is rhyolite, the most common rock in Yellowstone. Rhyolite erupted as flows of volcanic ash and hot gas.

Obsidian Cliff looks like black glass. Obsidian is the same kind of rock as rhyolite, but when it was lava it cooled more quickly than the lava that made rhyolite. The Indians used this dark glassy obsidian to make arrow points.

The columns of Sheepeater Cliffs are another kind of volcanic rock called basalt. Like rhyolite and obsidian, basalt left the volcano as melted rock, or lava. When the lava cooled, it turned into columns of brown rock with five and six flat sides.

Sheepeater Cliffs ▶

Petrified Forests

Interesting signs of volcanic eruptions are the petrified forests across the northern part of the park. You can see them at Specimen Ridge. It's near Tower Junction on the Northeast Entrance Road.

Scientists are still studying these petrified trees. Many of the standing trees were buried by ash or by volcanic mudflows such as those that occurred at Mount St. Helens in the 1980s. Some of the trees were carried from higher ground to the Lamar River area. As thousands of years passed, the trees slowly turned to stone. Fossilized by time, they now stand silent.

Petrified wood may **NOT** be collected in Yellowstone National Park. But you *can* buy a permit at the Gardiner Ranger District in Montana to collect it in Gallatin National Forest.

When you visit Yellowstone's Specimen Ridge, you might wonder what secrets these petrified trees still hide within their rings. Perhaps one day you will be a geologist who discovers a few more facts to help answer some of the many questions we still have about the petrified forests of Yellowstone.

Petrified Trees

What Secrets Hide Within This Petrified Wood?

Grand Canyon of the Yellowstone

Along with later volcanoes came three ice ages. At those times, much of the park area was covered with sheets of ice called glaciers. These huge chunks of ice moved down the mountainsides. One of the melting glaciers formed Yellowstone Lake.

Huge floods from bursting glacier dams carved the Grand Canyon of the Yellowstone. Through this deep, yellow rock canyon, the Yellowstone River rushes and drops 109 feet at the Upper Fall. Another drop of 308 feet makes the famous Lower Fall.

The rock of the canyon is rhyolite, but hot water and gases have turned this rhyolite soft and yellow.

At Canyon Village Visitor Center, you can see displays, talk to Park Rangers, and find out how to get to the safest and best places to see the falls. Favorite places are Inspiration Point, Grand View, Lookout Point, and Artist Point.

Lower Yellowstone Fall ►

Hot Springs

The earth is a giant ball with a hard or solid core in the center. Around the center core are layers of hot melted rock called magma. We live on the hard, outer part, the crust. In Yellowstone, the earth's crust is thin in spots, where the magma is only three kilometers beneath the surface. Magma heats rocks in the crust and acts as a giant water heater. Water from rain and melting snow soaks into the ground. When this water gets hot, it makes the different kinds of hot, or thermal, features you see in Yellowstone.

One thermal feature is the hot spring. Its hot water rises to the surface through cracks in the ground. As the hot water bubbles up, it washes minerals from the rocks below and brings them to the surface. When the water cools and releases gases, minerals are left behind. The minerals build up and make steps, or terraces, like Minerva and Jupiter Terraces at Mammoth Hot Springs.

Some hot springs, like Morning Glory Pool in Upper Geyser Basin, do not build terraces.

Minerva Terrace

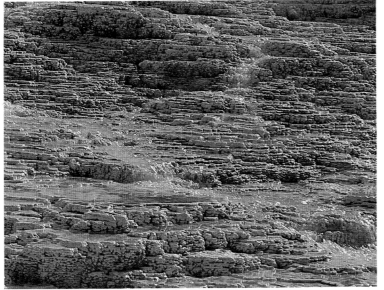

Jupiter Terrace

Morning Glory Pool

Another thermal feature is the geyser. Yellowstone has thousands of geysers, but only about 500 have names. Some geysers spout, or erupt, every now and then. Others can almost be predicted. Old Faithful got its name because it erupts fairly regularly and faithfully. The spout is 106 to 184 feet high.

It takes three things to make a geyser: water, heat, and a strong set of holes and cracks in the ground called a plumbing

Geysers

system. Water from snow and rain gets into the plumbing system and gets hot from the magma. Then it rises in the plumbing system. Steam bubbles form, grow bigger, and rise. These bubbles push the upper, cooler water out of the geyser. This lets pressure off the very hot water farther down. Like the water in a pressure cooker, it turns to steam so fast that it shoots to the surface and into the air.

Old Faithful erupts every 50 to 100 minutes, but it's fun to try to predict exactly when this famous geyser will erupt. If an eruption is short, the next one will be sooner. A long eruption usually means Old Faithful needs more time to build up steam and pressure before the next eruption.

Old Faithful ►

Geyser Basins

Geyser basins are places where enough heat, water, and plumbing systems come together to form many thermal features. The plumbing systems are fragile and can easily be destroyed if *anything* is thrown into them.

Like the water in a hot spring, the water under a geyser washes minerals from the underground rocks. These minerals come to the surface along with the water. When the water cools, it leaves deposits of minerals. These built-up mounds are called cones. Grotto Geyser in the Upper Geyser Basin has a cone with a very strange shape.

Midway Geyser Basin sends many cloud puffs into the air beside the Firehole River.

In the Black Sand Basin, Punch Bowl Spring brings its minerals up to build a beautiful cone.

CAUTION: Thin crusts and boiling water make walking around geysers, mudpots, and hot springs very dangerous. The Park Service has built walkways for your safety. Use them to avoid serious accidents!

Grotto Geyser Has A Strangely Shaped Cone

Midway Geyser Basin

Punch Bowl Spring

Fumaroles

Thermal features look and sound strange. They even smell strange. The smells come from gases that rise with the water and steam.

Holes or vents with steam and gas coming out are called *fumaroles*. You can usually see fumaroles on hillsides or high ground like the ones on Roaring Mountain. This mountain got its name in 1902 when the vents became very active and roared like a monster. But since then the vents have grown bigger. The steam can come out without making so much noise and Roaring Mountain only snores.

But even when it's snoring, Roaring Mountain is exciting to see on frosty mornings. The cold air makes thick fluffy clouds of steam. During the winter, when snow covers the nearby mountains, Roaring Mountain melts the snow that falls on it. So there it sits, bare, warm, and steamy. It sounds like a snoring monster asleep in the snow. When you look at fumaroles, stay on the walks so you won't step into the monster's many mouths.

Roaring Mountain ►

Mudpots

Near the west entrance of the park on the Grand Loop Road, you can go on a boardwalk to the Fountain Paint Pots. Stay on the boardwalk and walk a half-mile loop to all kinds of thermal features.

The Fountain Paint Pots are mudpots that bubble and gurgle. Sometimes the bubbles get as big as basketballs. When they burst, the mudpots send out hot globs and stringy lumps.

A mudpot is much like a fumarole except that it has a bowl-like place where steam, rain, and melted snow collect. The water mixes with clay and minerals to make a mixture like thick paint. It may be gray, black, white, or cream colored. When iron is one of the minerals, the mud gets pink or red.

Gas rises to the surface and makes bubbles that burst and give off a smell like rotten eggs.

Near Monument Geyser Basin, the Artist Paint Pots are all colors. The Chocolate Pots across the Gibbon River from there look tasty, but no one eats them!

Mudpot ▶

Life in Hot Water

Many thermal features have beautiful colors. A few colors come from minerals in the water. Most colors come from tiny plants called algae that grow in warm or cold water.

In very hot water, no algae can grow. But as the water flows away and cools, it may provide a home for some algae which are yellow green to orange to dark green.

Algae are the start of a food chain. Many tiny animals feed on them. One of the links in the food chain is the brine fly and its larvae. The brine fly and other insects eat the algae. Then the insects and brine fly are eaten by spiders and beetles. Dragon flies eat the spiders and tiny insects.

Birds feast on flies, insects, and other animals that live in the warm water. Bigger birds and mammals eat smaller birds and mammals. This is one of many food chains that exist in all kinds of wildlife.

You can see how algae grow at the Grand Prismatic Spring in Midway Geyser Basin. Others are at pools and springs in the West Thumb thermal basin.

Grand Prismatic Spring ▶

—and More Life

Yellowstone ground heat helps many plants bloom early. During June, deep blue-violet fringed gentian blooms in geyser basins where the earth is warm.

There are hundreds of kinds of flowers in Yellowstone, from fireweed to cactus, wild iris, blue flax, and mountain hollyhock. The Wyoming state flower, Indian paintbrush, splashes the mountain slopes red. Montana's state flower, the bitterroot, and Idaho's sego lily also grow in Yellowstone.

Summer beauty that blooms in Yellowstone will last forever in a picture you draw or take with your camera. But if you pick a flower, it dies quickly and is gone forever. When you pick a blossom, it cannot produce the seeds that will fall to the ground where they can sprout and grow the following year.

At Yellowstone National Park, you can do many things to preserve the natural wonders that may greet *your* children and grandchildren in the years to come.

Bitterroot—Montana State Flower

Sego Lily—Idaho State Flower

Yellowstone's Flower—Fringed Gentian

Paintbrush—Wyoming State Flower

Trees

Most of Yellowstone Park is covered by forests of lodgepole pine. Millions of these trees are being killed by mountain pine beetles. The trees turn orange as the needles die. This is a natural process that thins the forest and allows more sunlight and water to reach the ground. The trees become food sources and homes for many animals. Decaying trees become part of the soil. This is a never-ending cycle of life and death.

Where Douglas-fir grows, the spruce budworm brings about a similar cycle.

While you're in the park, you may see smoke that says *forest fire*. Does it surprise you to know that many of these fires are allowed to burn? Fires are another natural way forests are renewed. Forests of mixed ages, some very old and some recently burned, offer homes for more kinds of animals.

Fire also promotes the growth of new quaking aspen trees by removing the old trees and making sun and nutrients available to their sprouts. Since the smallest breeze makes the quaking aspen's leaves shake, they shimmer green in the summer and gold in the fall.

Lodgepole Pines At Sylvan Lake

Aspen in Autumn

Bison

Some call it the American buffalo, but it's really the bison. This animal is bigger than a horse. Woolly fur covers its head, shoulders, and front legs. For some Indian people, the bison was the most important animal in their lives. They killed buffalo for meat and used the skins for robes and tipis.

In 1859, tens of thousands of buffalo still roamed the center of North America. But when the railroads came to this area, hunters arrived on the scene and hunted the bison as it had never been hunted before. One man with a rifle could shoot more bison in a short time than a whole tribe of Indians could kill in a year. By 1889, there were only 700 left. But a small herd was protected in Yellowstone National Park. Now a wild herd of about 2,000 bison ranges freely over the park.

In summer, most of Yellowstone's bison go to the high country, but a few can be seen in the Lower Geyser Basin meadows and in Hayden Valley. During winter, buffalo can live in deep snow. With their great heads, they sweep the snow aside to reach grass to eat. Some stay near the thermal areas to save their energy.

Trumpeter Swan

Another animal Yellowstone helped save from extinction is the Trumpeter Swan. This water bird, or waterfowl, can have a wingspan of 8 feet. Its huge wingspan and trumpet sound once filled the sky between Alaska and Mexico. But in 1932 there were fewer than 70 of these waterfowl to be counted. Their beautiful feathers had been turned into powder puffs, feather decorations, and stuffing for pillows and quilts.

Later, a few Trumpeter Swans came to nest just outside Yellowstone's west boundary in the Red Rock Lakes of Montana. This area was then made a refuge where animals could be safe.

By 1969, there were 4 or 5 thousand Trumpeter Swans in the country and 15 pairs stayed all year in Yellowstone.

Every year, each pair of swans hatched 6 cygnets. But by the 1970s, they only hatched 3 cygnets a year. Now people are afraid that the graceful white Trumpeter Swan may become extinct.

Trumpeter Swan ►

Predators

Animals that kill other animals for food are called *predators*. For a long time people said, "Predators are bad."

In Yellowstone's early days, predators like cougars, wolves, and coyotes were hunted or poisoned to protect the elk and other "good" animals. But when humans protect one kind of animal or another, they upset a balance that existed in wildlife before people came into the picture.

Today many people believe that predators are not bad. Wildlife gets along better if we don't try to get rid of certain animals or plants.

In Yellowstone, there are a few cougars that hide in the high country. But you can see coyotes if you look in the sagebrush and watch for them along riverbanks.

Other predators protected by the park are wolverines, bobcats, and lynx. Now we know these predators are an important part of wildlife and nature.

Coyote ►

Bears

Everyone who visits Yellowstone National Park hopes to see bears and their young. This park is home for many black bears and a few grizzlies. The grizzly bear is king of the mountain.

For many years after the park was established, grizzlies and black bears learned to live partly on food from garbage dumps and food left around by careless campers. Over a forty-year period, about 2,000 visitors were hurt, and a lot of property was damaged by bears.

Then the dumps and campgrounds were cleaned up. Garbage-eating bears were removed but many kept causing trouble and had to be destroyed. During that time 953 black bears and 126 grizzlies had to be killed.

You can help park rangers keep the bears from being killed by not letting bears get too dependent on human foods. **DO NOT FEED ANY ANIMALS IN THE PARK.**

Black Bears Are Sometimes Brown ▶

Other Animals

Yellowstone National Park is truly an animal refuge, a place where animals live and die naturally. People do not hunt animals in the park. Laws protect native fishes, the cutthroat trout and Montana grayling. White pelicans, ospreys, otters, and grizzlies need these fish to eat.

Protected animals do not overpopulate the park because their numbers are limited in natural ways. During winter, old and weak elk and bison die in the snowy cold. Then in the spring, they become food for bears, coyotes, eagles, magpies, and ravens.

Natural fires renew the forest and create new homes for bluebirds in burned stumps.

From the largest moose to the smallest insect, all animals, even the cricket and the pesky mosquito, have a place in the total balance of life in the wild.

Look for animals in the places they like: moose in willows, bison in wet meadows, deer in the sagebrush, pronghorns on open hills. Look up to the steep slopes, cliffs, or ridges to find bighorn sheep, and watch nearly everywhere for elk.

Moose

Butterfly

Elk

Mormon Cricket

Redwing Blackbird

Yellowstone Yesterday

The first non-Indian people to see Yellowstone were trappers like John Colter and Jim Bridger. Since Bridger was known for wild and tall tales, few people believed the stories he told of a place "where Hell bubbled up." Burning plains? Immense lakes? Boiling springs? Who could believe such things?

In 1870, a group from Montana explored this land of wonder. Then the U.S. government sent a team to study and map the area. Their photographs, sketches, and geological specimens were shown at the capitol in Washington while Congress considered bills to make Yellowstone a public park.

A bill to set Yellowstone aside for the enjoyment of people was passed, and on March 1, 1872, President Grant signed it. This area became the first national park in the world.

Soon hundreds of people came to the park by horse and buggy, stagecoach, wagon, bicycle, and finally by car. Today you can find out what a bumpy ride those early visitors endured to get to Yellowstone. At Roosevelt near Tower Junction, you can take a ride in an old stagecoach pulled by horses.

Stagecoach Ride

Yellowstone for You

You would have to spend years in Yellowstone Park to see and do everything. At every stop, Park Rangers are ready to help and answer questions. They also offer programs that make a visit to Yellowstone have more meaning.

At Old Faithful, you can go geyser gazing with a Ranger. You'll see little known geysers and hear how they work.

Almost all points in the park have evening programs with slides and talks.

There is a climb through time at the Petrified Forest. Or you can visit the Old Fort Yellowstone army barracks with an old-time soldier.

On the Three Senses Trail, you close your eyes and follow a fence. While you walk, you use three senses: hearing, smelling, and feeling. You hear the wind in the trees and the gurgles of thermal features. You smell gases and feel steamy, warm ground and wet grass.

Through all your senses, feel yourself to be part of this amazing place which has existed for millions of years.

Park Rangers Tell How And Why

Three Senses Trail

Yellowstone Sports

You can make up your own things to do at Yellowstone. Horseback trips and backpacking are great because you get to parts of the park where cars cannot go. There are many places to fish. You can fish from a big or small rented boat at Yellowstone Lake. You can take a boat to places on the lake where you can camp and fish.

Whatever you choose to do, you will leave Yellowstone wishing you could stay longer. You may decide to come back next year.

You'll leave with many thanks to the rangers, the trees, the waterfalls. You can thank the people who knew that some day you would come here. And you'll thank the millions of visitors who helped to keep the park beautiful for your visit.

Now it's your turn to enjoy the wonders of Yellowstone National Park. It's your turn to leave its beauty for the millions of visitors still to come.

Lamar River Trail

Firehole River

Canoeing—Yellowstone Lake

Upper Geyser Basin

Other National Parks in Wyoming and Montana

GRAND TETON NATIONAL PARK in Wyoming is not far from Yellowstone National Park. This park is known for its huge mountain peaks. It's a place to camp, hike, fish, and climb mountains. In the winter, skiers dot the snowy slopes at Jackson Hole Ski Area at Teton Village.

GLACIER NATIONAL PARK in Montana is often called the "outdoors-person's park." Glacier is joined with Canada's Waterton National Park as Glacier-Waterton International Peace Park. It is also a Biosphere Reserve, a place where people study relationships among plants, animals, people, and climate in a constant state of change.

There are more than a thousand miles of well-marked trails and good campsites in Glacier National Park. It's also an interesting place to see huge moving chunks of ice called glaciers.

Many lakes, towering peaks, and unusual birds and plants make Glacier National Park one big BEQUEST OF BEAUTY.

Grand Teton National Park, Wyoming

Glacier National Park, Montana

About the Author and Illustrator

Wyoming-born Ruth Radlauer's love affair with nature and national parks began in Wyoming where she spent her summers at camp on Casper Mountain or traveling with her family in Yellowstone National Park.

Mr. and Mrs. Radlauer, graduates of the University of California at Los Angeles, are authors of many books for young people of all ages. Their subjects range from robots to radio and volcanoes to coral reefs.

Photographing the national parks is a labor of love for Rolf Zillmer and his wife Evelyn. The Zillmers get an intimate view of each park, since they are backpack and wildlife enthusiasts.

A former student at Art Center College of Design in Los Angeles, Mr. Zillmer is a fine sculptor of wildlife cast in bronze. He was born in New York City and now makes his home in California where he is the Art Director for Elk Grove Books.